FUN & EASY ORIGAMI

Packed with Paper-Folding Projects!

ARCTURUS

ARCTURUS

This edition published in 2015 by Arcturus Publishing Limited
26/27 Bickels Yard, 151–153 Bermondsey Street,
London SE1 3HA

ISBN: 978-1-78404-787-0
CH004401NT
Supplier: 26, Date 0514, Print run 4061

Models and photography by Michael Wiles
Written by Catherine Ard
Designed by Emma Randall and Belinda Webster
Additional design elements from Shutterstock
Edited by Joe Harris and Frances Evans
Cartoon artworks by Joe Harris

Printed in China

Contents

SPEEDY DELIVERIES

Introduction

Origami is a Japanese art form that has been popular for hundreds of years. In traditional origami, models are made from one sheet of folded paper. There is no cutting, gluing, or drawing!

In this book, we have broken the rules a little, because we thought it would be fun to decorate our finished projects. If you would like to do so too, you will need to use scissors to cut out paper eyes and other simple shapes. Glue them to your models, and then decorate them with marker pens.

Basic Folds

The paper used in origami is thin, but strong, so that it can be folded many times. It is usually white on one side. Alternatively you can use ordinary scrap paper, but make sure it's not too thick.

Origami models often share the same folds and basic designs. This introduction explains some of the folds that you will need for the projects in this book. When making the models, follow the key below to find out what the lines and arrows mean. And always crease well!

KEY

valley fold - - - - - - - - - - - - - - step fold (mountain and   direction to move paper ↘

mountain fold ••••••••••••• valley fold next to each other)   push ▼   hold ☞

MOUNTAIN FOLD

To make a mountain fold, fold the paper so that the crease is pointing up at you, like a mountain.

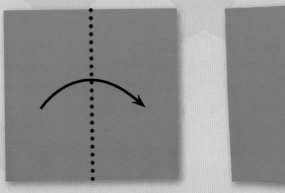

VALLEY FOLD

To make a valley fold, fold the paper the other way, so that the crease is pointing away from you, like a valley.

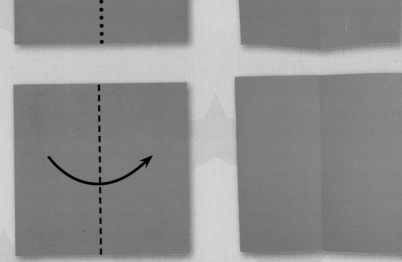

INSIDE REVERSE FOLD

An inside reverse fold is useful if you want to make a nose or a tail, or if you want to flatten off the shape of another part of an origami model.

1 First fold a piece of paper diagonally in half. Make a valley fold on one point and crease.

2 It's important to make sure that the paper is creased well. Run your finger over the crease two or three times.

3 Unfold and open up the corner slightly. Refold the crease nearest to you into a mountain fold.

open

4 Open up the paper a little more and then tuck the tip of the point inside. Close the paper. This is the view from the underside of the paper.

5 Flatten the paper. You now have an inside reverse fold.

OUTSIDE REVERSE FOLD

An outside reverse fold is useful if you want to make a head, beak, foot, or another part of your model that sticks out.

1 First fold a piece of paper diagonally in half. Make a valley fold on one point and crease.

2 It's important to make sure that the paper is creased well. Run your finger over the crease two or three times.

3 Unfold and open up the corner slightly. Refold the crease farthest away from you into a valley fold.

Open

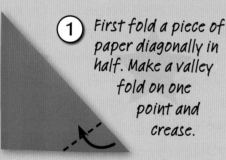

4 Open up the paper a little more and start to turn the corner inside out. Then close the paper when the fold begins to turn.

5 You now have an outside reverse fold. You can either flatten the paper or leave it rounded out.

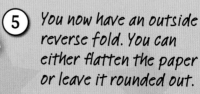

Origami in
SPACE

Rocket

Easy

There's a thundering roar as the rocket fuel bursts into flames. 5-4-3-2-1... LIFTOFF! Start your own incredible space mission with this cool origami rocket.

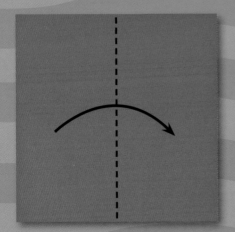

1. Place the paper as shown. Fold it in half from left to right and unfold.

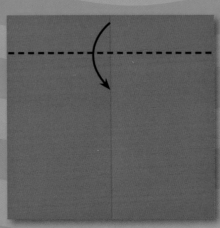

2. Valley fold a wide strip along the top edge.

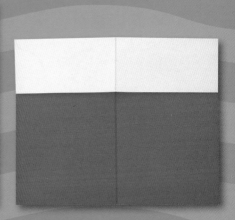

3. Turn the paper over.

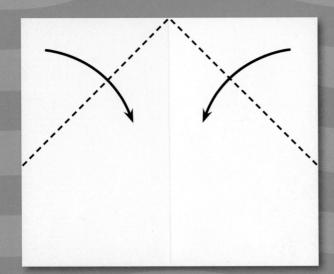

4. Valley fold the top corners to meet the middle crease.

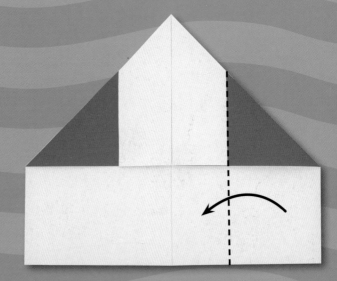

5. Valley fold the right side in line with the edge of the red triangle, as shown.

Did You Know?

The first space explorers were animals. Monkeys, mice, cats, and dogs were all sent into space before astronauts.

6 Valley fold the right side again.

7 Now valley fold the left side in line with the edge of the red triangle.

8 Valley fold the left side again so both sides match.

9 Open up the inner corner of the right flap and valley fold the top layer.

10 Press the paper flat.

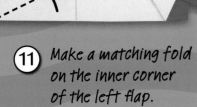

11 Make a matching fold on the inner corner of the left flap.

12 Turn the model over.

14 Draw some spacemen on your rocket, then begin the countdown to liftoff!

13 Your finished project should look like this.

Robot

Whether they are roaming around Mars or collecting rock samples from the Moon, robots are perfectly at home in space. Fold this little robot so he's ready to explore a new planet!

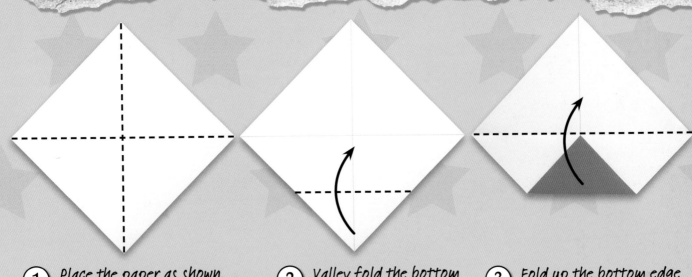

1. Place the paper as shown. Valley fold the paper in half one way and unfold, then the other way and unfold.

2. Valley fold the bottom corner so the point meets the crease in the middle.

3. Fold up the bottom edge along the central crease.

4. Your paper should look like this. Turn the paper over.

5. Valley fold the left point onto the right side.

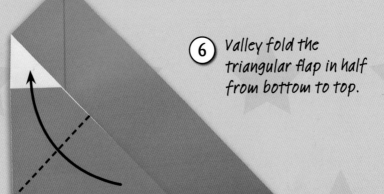

6. Valley fold the triangular flap in half from bottom to top.

(7) Fold down the top point of the flap as shown.

(8) Now valley fold the right point onto the left side.

(9) Valley fold the triangular flap in half from bottom to top.

(10) Fold down the top point of the flap to match the other side.

(11) Fold down the point at the top.

Did You Know?

Robonaut is the robot used on the International Space Station. He has arms, legs, and five-fingered hands, so he can help out the crew with difficult jobs!

(12) Valley fold the tips of the top corners.

(13) Fold over a strip along the bottom of the model.

(14) Make angled valley folds to the top corners of the strip. These are the legs.

(15) Turn your model over.

(16) Your finished project should look like this.

(17) Draw a friendly face on your robot. Why not stick him on a piece of paper and add some antennae!

UFO

Could this mysterious spacecraft be carrying alien visitors from distant planets? Choose a dark shade of paper and fold a flying saucer to hover in the night sky.

① Start with a square of paper, white side up. Fold it in half from left to right and unfold.

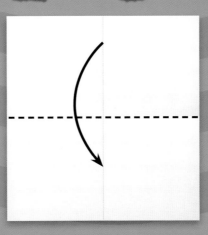

② Fold it in half from top to bottom.

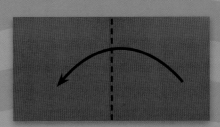

③ Now fold the paper in half from right to left to make a square.

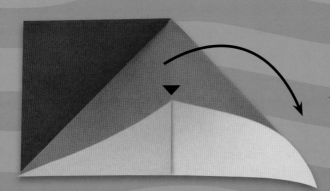

④ Open up the top layer and pull the corner to the right. Press down on the top and flatten the paper to make a triangle.

⑤ Turn the paper over.

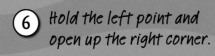

⑥ Hold the left point and open up the right corner.

OPEN

7 Pull the top layer over so that the corner meets the left point. Flatten the paper to make a triangle.

8 Valley fold the top layer of the left and right points to meet on the middle crease.

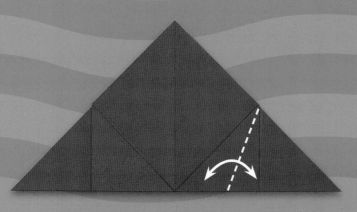

9 Valley fold the right flap so that the outside edge lines up with the inside edge. Unfold and open up the point, then flatten it into a kite shape.

10 Do the same on the other side. These are the jets for the UFO.

Did You Know?

In 1947, a pilot saw nine UFOs in the sky.
He said they moved like saucers skipping on water.
The name "flying saucers" has been used ever since!

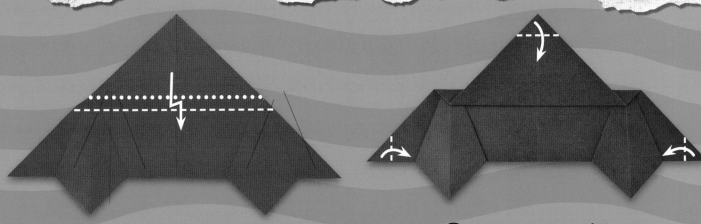

11 Make a step fold across the middle of the model.

12 Fold in the tips of the points.

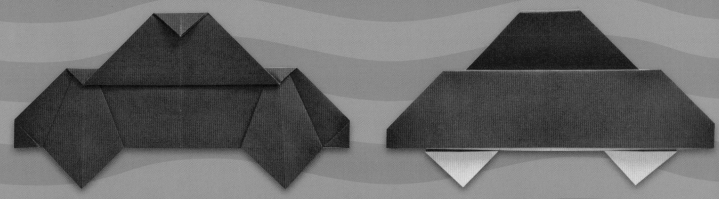

13 Turn the model over.

14 Your finished project should look like this.

15 Draw some alien explorers on your spacecraft. Now your UFO is ready to beam up some earthlings!

Galaxy

There are billions of galaxies in the universe, each one made up of trillions of stars and planets. Use some yellow paper to fold this spiral of brightly glowing stars.

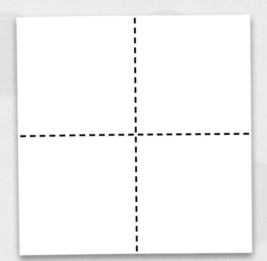

1 Place the paper as shown and fold it in half from top to bottom and unfold, then from left to right and unfold.

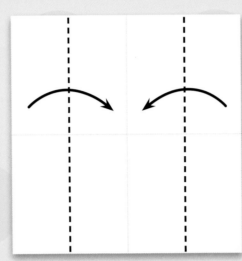

2 Valley fold the sides to meet the central crease.

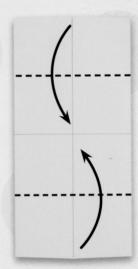

3 Valley fold the top and bottom to meet in the middle.

4 Completely unfold the paper.

5 Valley fold the paper diagonally from corner to corner one way and unfold, then from corner to corner the other way and unfold.

Did You Know?

Earth, the Sun, and all of the planets in our solar system sit inside a galaxy called the Milky Way. It contains up to 400 billion stars!

⑥ Your paper should look like this.

⑦ Pinch the top right corner and fold in the top and the right side along the creases. Flatten the paper.

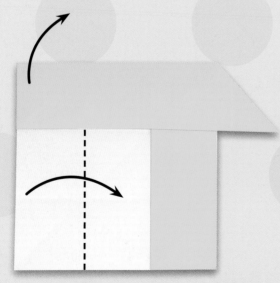

⑧ Pull out the top left corner, then fold in the left side. Flatten the paper.

⑨ Your paper should look like this. Turn the paper upside down.

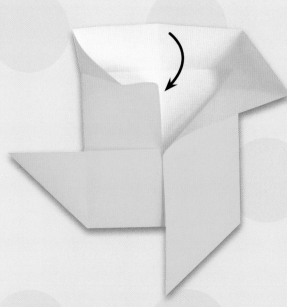

10 Pull out the top right corner and fold down the top edge.

11 Unfold the top left corner and pull out the point. Fold down the top edge and flatten the model into shape.

12 Your finished project should look like this.

13 Your spiral galaxy is ready to spin through space!

Alien

Some people believe that there are strange creatures living in space. Prepare for some otherworldly origami when you fold this spooky alien face!

1. Start with the white side facing up. Fold the paper in half from left to right and unfold.

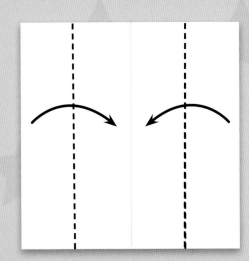

2. Valley fold the sides to meet the middle crease.

3. Valley fold the inner points to meet the outside edges.

4. Valley fold the top right corner and unfold again.

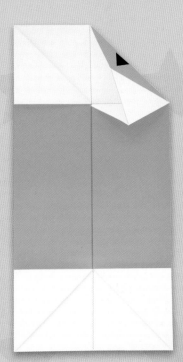

5. Open up the flap and push the corner point over to meet the central crease. Flatten the paper.

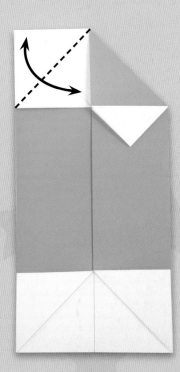

6. Repeat steps 4 and 5 on the other side. The white triangles are the alien's eyes.

7 Mountain fold the point at the top.

8 Valley fold the white section.

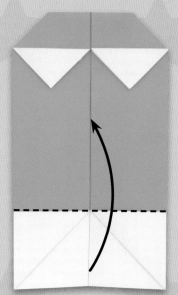

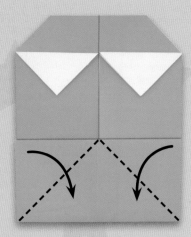

9 Valley fold the top corners of the flap to meet in the middle of the bottom edge.

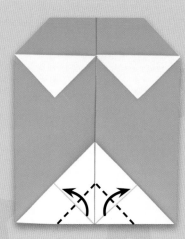

10 Valley fold the inner points to meet the white edges.

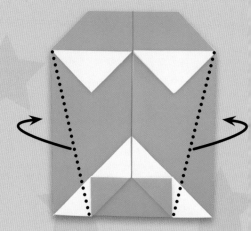

11 Make angled mountain folds on either side to shape the face.

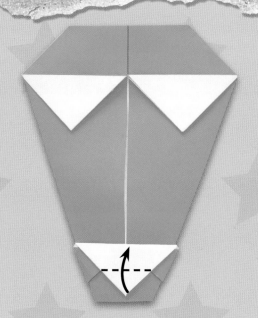

(12) Fold down the white triangle.

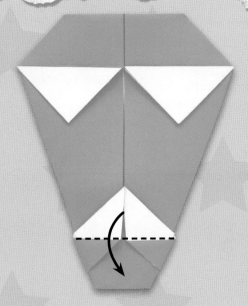

(13) Fold the tip of the triangle up. This is the alien's jaw.

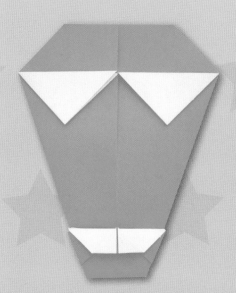

(14) Your finished project should look like this.

(15) Draw some beady eyes, a nose, and a mouth. Let's hope this extraterrestrial comes in peace!

Space Shuttle

It took a lot of time, money, and a team of top scientists to send this awesome, reusable spacecraft into orbit. You can launch a space shuttle in a matter of minutes with a few cosmic folds!

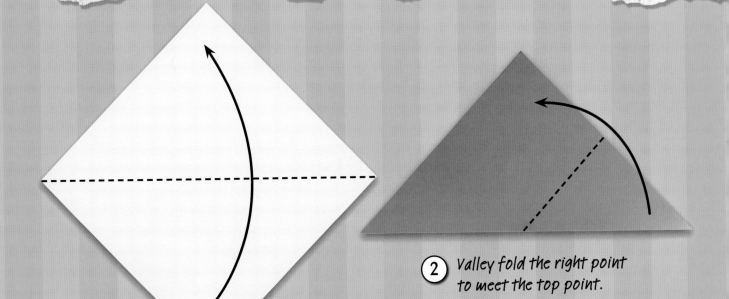

① Start with a square of paper, white side up, and with one point facing you. Valley fold in half from bottom to top.

② Valley fold the right point to meet the top point.

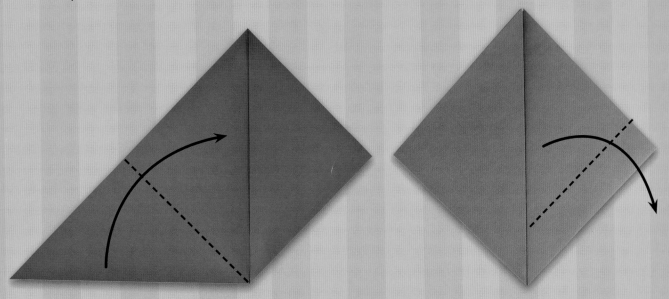

③ Valley fold the left point to meet the top point. This makes a square.

④ Make a valley fold on the right flap about 15 mm (1/2 in) from the bottom edge.

Did You Know?

While in orbit, the space shuttle flew around Earth at a speed of about 28,000 km/h (17,500 mph)!

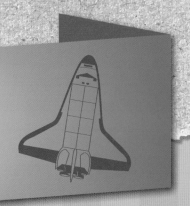

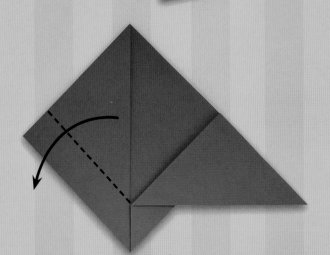

5 Now make a matching fold on the left flap.

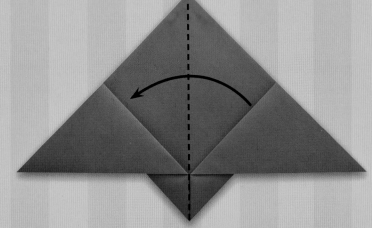

6 Valley fold the paper in half from right to left.

TAIL

NOSE

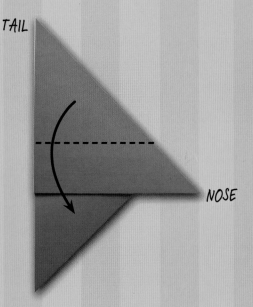

7 The top point will become the tail. Valley fold the tail to meet the bottom point.

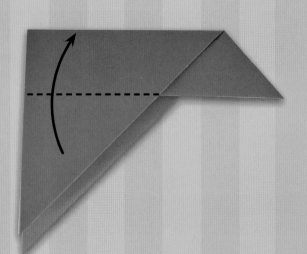

8 Fold the tail back up in line with the fold underneath.

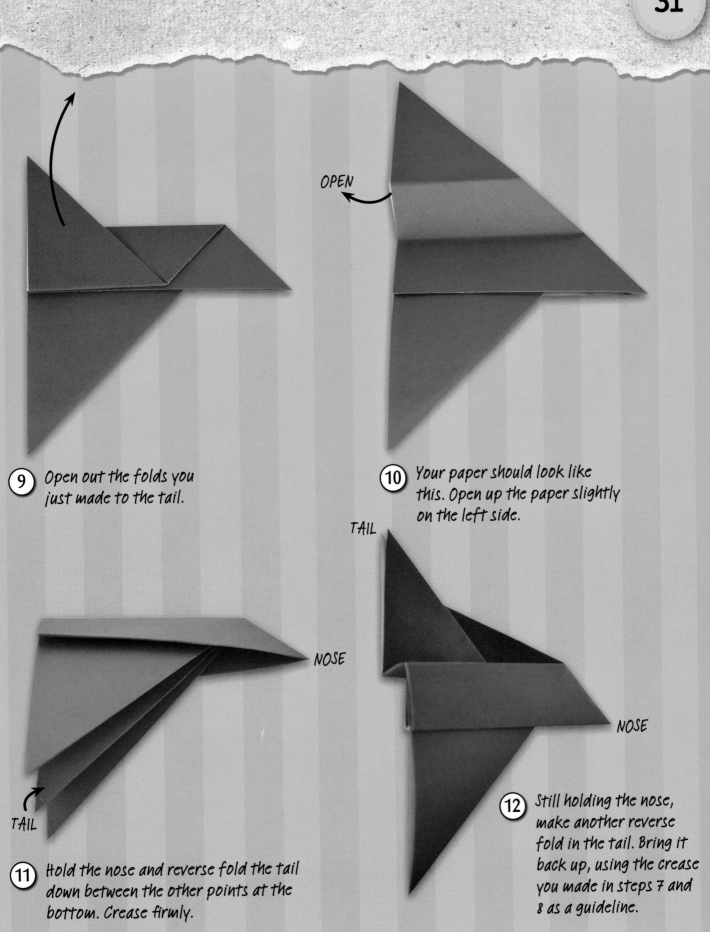

OPEN

9 Open out the folds you just made to the tail.

10 Your paper should look like this. Open up the paper slightly on the left side.

TAIL

NOSE

NOSE

TAIL

11 Hold the nose and reverse fold the tail down between the other points at the bottom. Crease firmly.

12 Still holding the nose, make another reverse fold in the tail. Bring it back up, using the crease you made in steps 7 and 8 as a guideline.

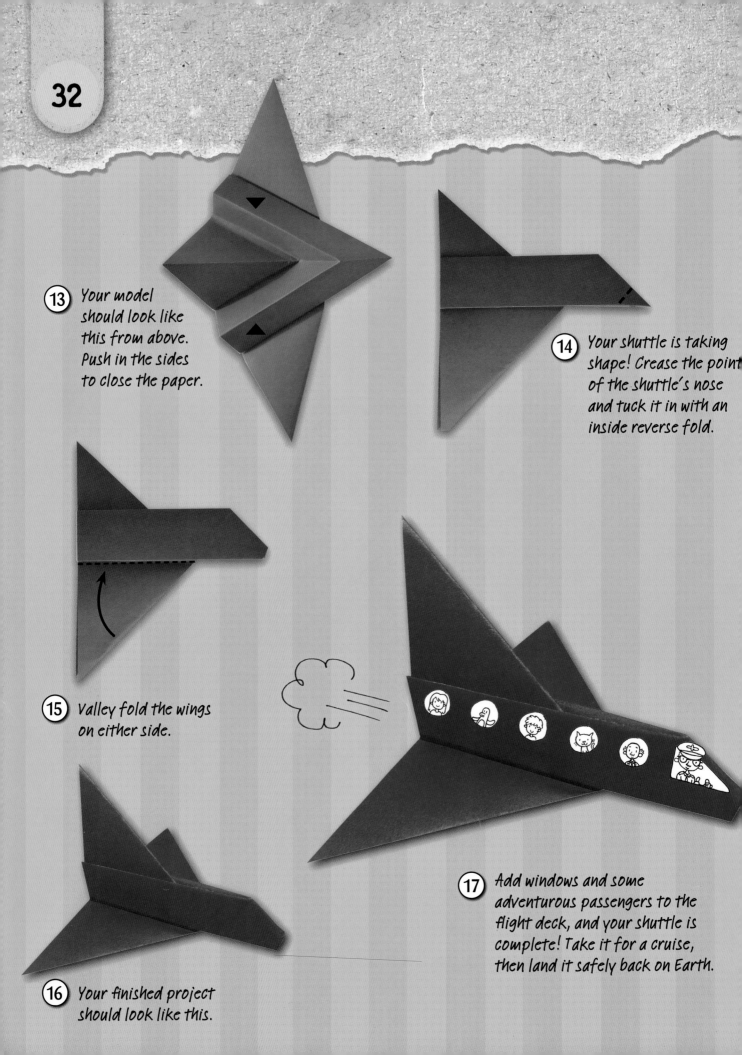

13 Your model should look like this from above. Push in the sides to close the paper.

14 Your shuttle is taking shape! Crease the point of the shuttle's nose and tuck it in with an inside reverse fold.

15 Valley fold the wings on either side.

16 Your finished project should look like this.

17 Add windows and some adventurous passengers to the flight deck, and your shuttle is complete! Take it for a cruise, then land it safely back on Earth.

Origami
BUGS

Ladybug

Ladybugs are not always red. Some ladybugs are orange, yellow, black, brown, or pink. Here's how to fold a cute red ladybug. You just need to add the spots!

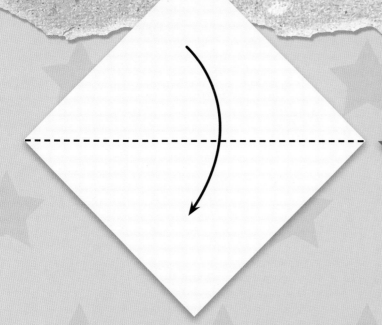

1. Start with a square of paper, white side up, and with one point facing you. Valley fold in half from top to bottom.

2. Valley fold the right point so it meets the bottom middle point.

3. Now valley fold the left point to meet the bottom middle point.

4. These are the wings. Turn your model over.

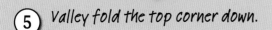

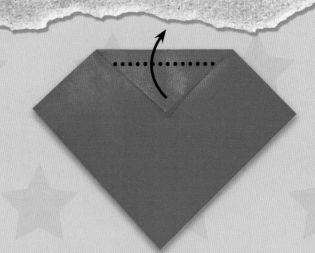

⑤ Valley fold the top corner down.

⑥ Mountain fold the flap back.

⑦ Valley fold the right corner.

⑧ Valley fold the left corner.

Did You Know?

Different types of ladybugs have different numbers of spots. Some have only two spots, while others have 24 spots… or more!

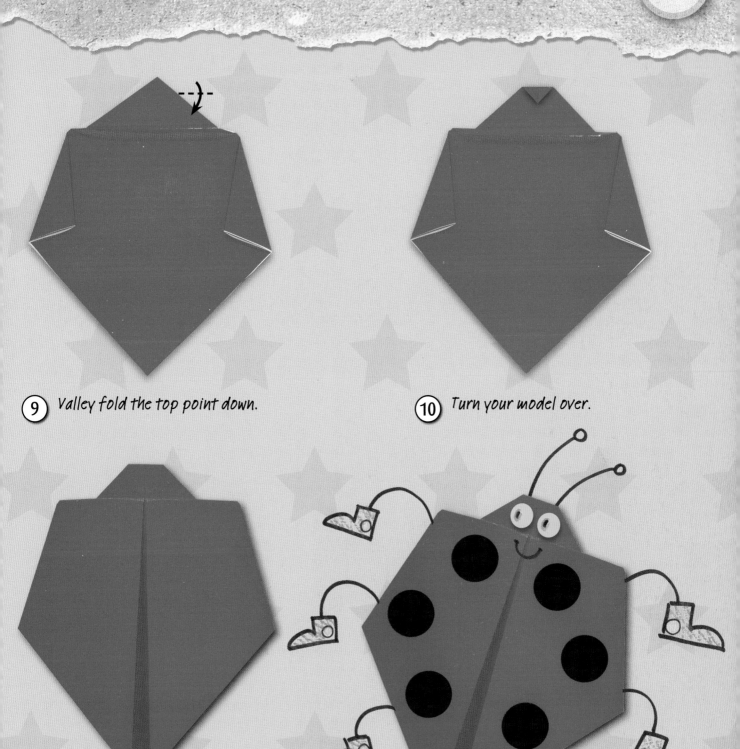

9. Valley fold the top point down.

10. Turn your model over.

11. Your finished project should look like this.

12. Draw some spots and a smiley face on your ladybug. Why not stick her on a piece of paper and add her antennae and legs!

Stag Beetle

Stag beetles get their name from their gigantic jaws, which look like the antlers on a deer. They use their jaws to wrestle rival stag beetles, not to hurt humans!

1 With the white side facing up, fold the paper from top to bottom and unfold, then from left to right and unfold.

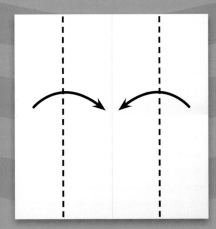

2 Valley fold the sides to meet the middle crease.

3 Now valley fold the top and bottom edges to meet in the middle.

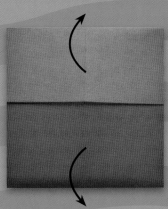

4 Open out the folds you made in step 3.

5 Valley fold the top corners to meet the first crease from the top.

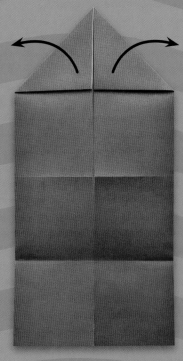

6 Unfold the corners.

Did You Know?

Stag beetle larvae are good for your garden because they eat up lots of rotting wood, but never touch living plants.

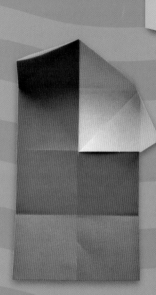

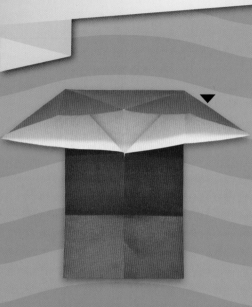

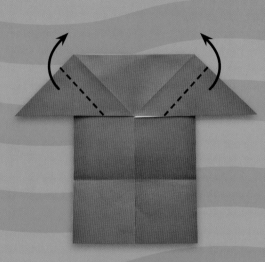

7 Open up the top layer on the right and fold it down to meet the central crease.

8 Repeat on the left side. Press down on the top to flatten the paper.

9 Valley fold the points to make two new triangles. Their points should stick straight up.

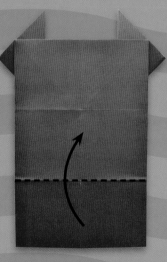

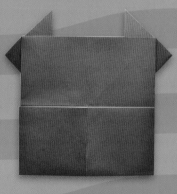

10 These points make the beetle's "antlers". Turn the paper over.

11 Fold in the bottom section along the crease, as shown.

12 Turn the paper over.

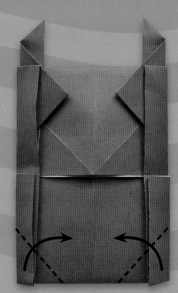

13 Fold in the sides, lining them up with the inside edges of the triangles.

14 Valley fold the bottom corners.

15 Turn the model over.

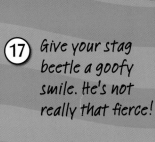

17 Give your stag beetle a goofy smile. He's not really that fierce!

16 Your finished project should look like this.

Bumblebee

Bumblebees are known for their bold stripes and fuzzy bodies. Get busy folding this friendly insect from yellow paper, then draw its black stripes with a pen.

① With one point facing you, fold the paper in half from top to bottom and unfold, then from left to right.

② Unfold the paper. Valley fold the top point around 40 mm (1 ½ in) above the central crease.

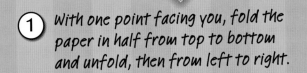

③ Mountain fold the right corner, lining up the yellow edge with the middle crease on the reverse.

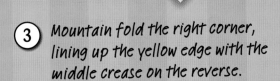

④ Mountain fold the left point in the same way.

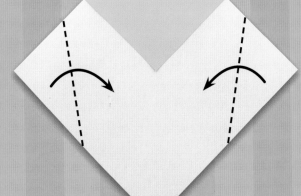

⑤ Valley fold the left and right corners as shown.

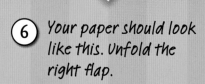

(6) Your paper should look like this. Unfold the right flap.

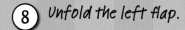

(7) Valley fold the corner tip so the edge meets the crease you made in step 5.

(8) Unfold the left flap.

(9) Valley fold the corner tip so the edge meets the crease you made in step 5.

(10) Unfold the right flap and open up the corner. Press it flat to make a triangle.

(11) Now do the same thing with the left flap.

(12) Valley fold the top point.

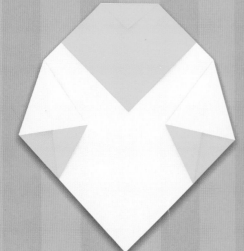

(13) Turn your model over.

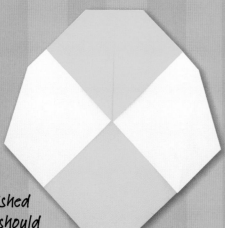

(14) Your finished project should look like this.

(15) Stick on eyes and draw black stripes across the body. Now your insect looks the bee's knees!

Caterpillar

Hard

Caterpillars nibble juicy leaves all day long! All that munching makes them big and strong, ready to change from a creepy-crawly into a fluttery butterfly or moth.

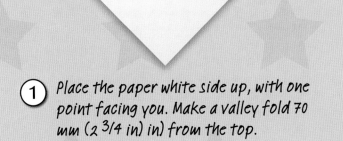

1. Place the paper white side up, with one point facing you. Make a valley fold 70 mm (2 3/4 in) in) from the top.

2. Now valley fold the bottom corner so that the point meets the top edge.

3. Turn the paper over.

6. Make a step fold on the right point. This is the caterpillar's tail.

5. Make another step fold about 30 mm (1 1/4 in) in from the folded edge.

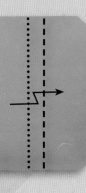

Did You Know?

A caterpillar has as many as 4,000 muscles in its tiny, wriggly body. The human body only has 629 muscles.

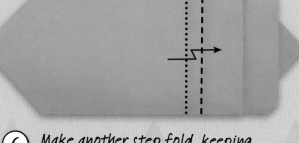

6 Make another step fold, keeping the folds an even distance apart.

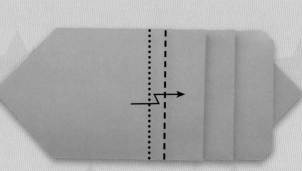

7 Continue with another step fold.

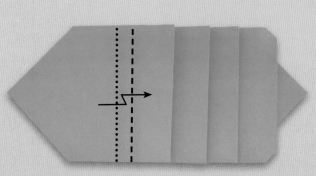

8 Make a final step fold. These folds are the sections of the caterpillar's body.

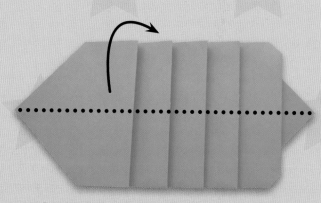

9 Mountain fold the paper in half.

10 Make an inside reverse fold on the left point. This is the head.

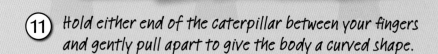

11 Hold either end of the caterpillar between your fingers and gently pull apart to give the body a curved shape.

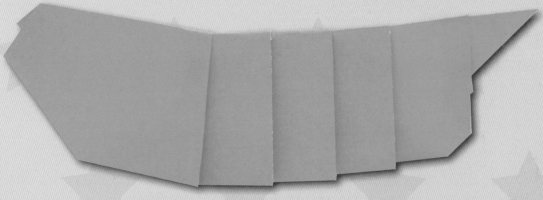

12 Your finished project should look like this.

13 Finish by drawing an eye on either side of the head and a friendly smile. Now place your origami caterpillar on a plant or a paper leaf ready to munch some lunch!

Butterfly

Butterflies have four delicate wings, which are often covered with bright patterns. Follow the steps to make a beautiful butterfly, ready to flutter to a flower.

1. With the white side facing up, valley fold the paper diagonally one way and unfold, then the other way.

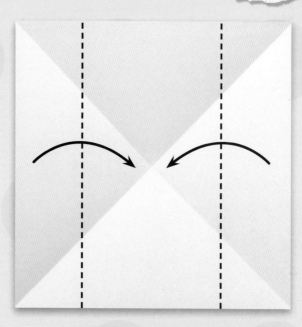

2. Unfold the paper. Valley fold the sides to meet in the middle.

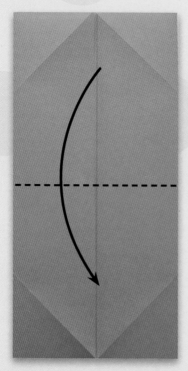

3. Fold in half and unfold.

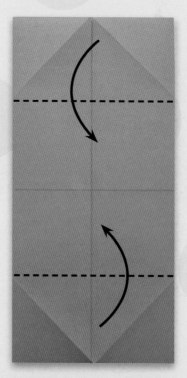

4. Valley fold the top and bottom to meet in the middle.

Did You Know?

A butterfly's mouth is like a long tube. It uses it to suck up nectar from flowers, sap from trees, or juices from fruit.

(5) Open up the top section.

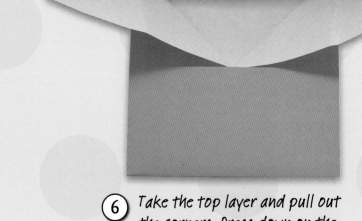

(6) Take the top layer and pull out the corners. Press down on the top to flatten the paper.

(7) You should now have this shape. Unfold the bottom section.

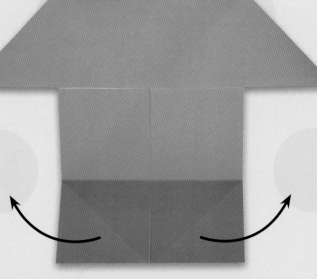

(8) Repeat step 5 with the other corners.

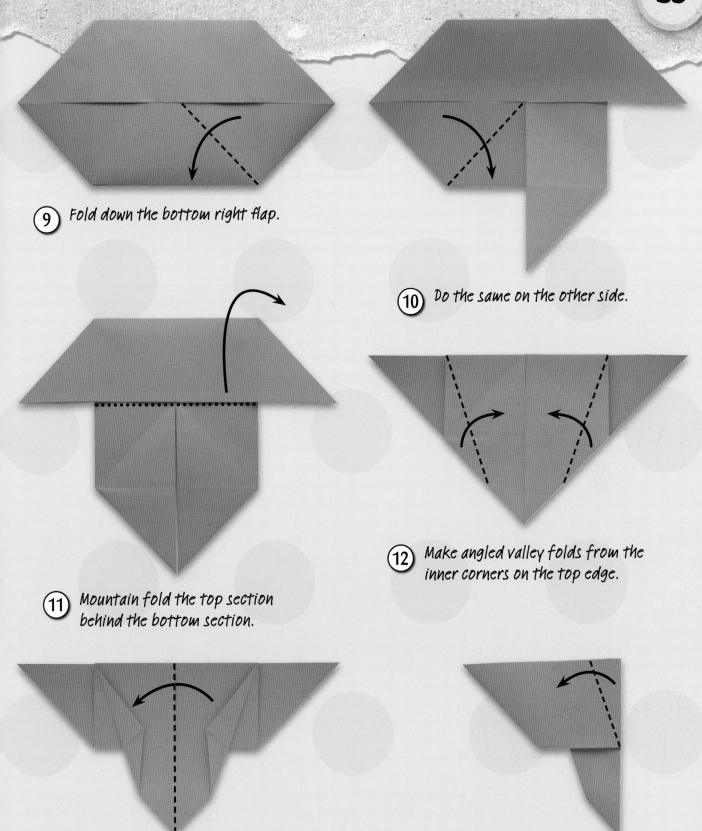

9 Fold down the bottom right flap.

10 Do the same on the other side.

11 Mountain fold the top section behind the bottom section.

12 Make angled valley folds from the inner corners on the top edge.

13 Valley fold the paper in half from right to left.

14 Make an angled valley fold across the right corner.

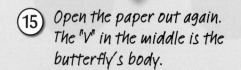

15 Open the paper out again. The "V" in the middle is the butterfly's body.

16 To make the body stick out, fold the left side across the right along the new crease.

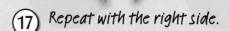

17 Repeat with the right side.

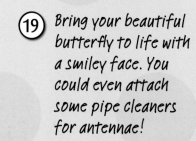

19 Bring your beautiful butterfly to life with a smiley face. You could even attach some pipe cleaners for antennae!

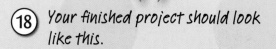

18 Your finished project should look like this.

Origami
MONSTERS

Frankenstein

Down in his secret laboratory, a mad scientist flicks a switch and his creepy creation shudders into life. Fold this fearsome Frankenstein face... if you dare!

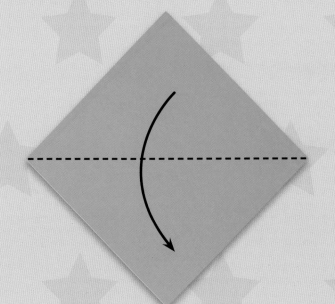

1 Place the paper as shown, with one point facing you. Valley fold in half from top to bottom, then unfold.

2 Valley fold the top corner so that the point meets the central crease.

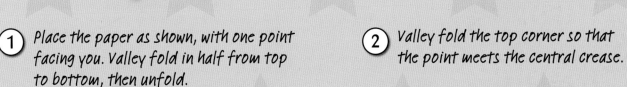

3 Make a crease about 15 mm (1/2 in) from the top and fold the point up again.

4 Fold the point back down to meet the edge of the last fold. This zigzag is Frankenstein's shaggy hair.

5 Make a step fold, starting with a valley fold just below the middle crease. This is the monster's forehead.

6 To shape the face, mountain fold the right side from the edge of the zigzag.

Did You Know?

In the original story by Mary Shelley, Frankenstein is the name of the monster's creator. The monster doesn't have a name.

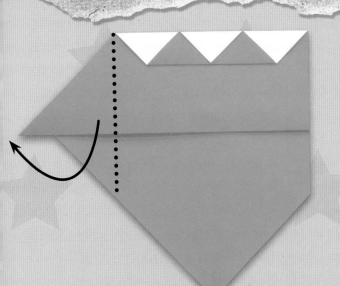

7 Mountain fold the left side in the same way.

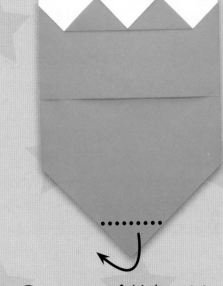

8 Mountain fold the point at the bottom to give your monster a square jaw.

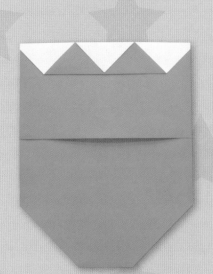

9 Your finished project should look like this.

10 Draw a sad mouth, eyes, and a scary scar to bring your monster to life. Why not fold a frightful girlfriend to keep your Frankenstein company?

Ghost

You don't need to hunt in haunted houses or creep about in graveyards in the dead of night. Fold this spooky model to see a paper ghost appear!

Use plain white origami paper, or pick a pale blue or yellow and start with the shaded side facing up.

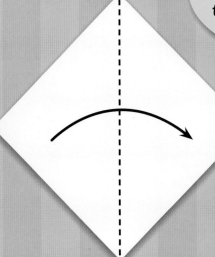

1. Place the paper with one point facing you. Valley fold in half from left to right and unfold.

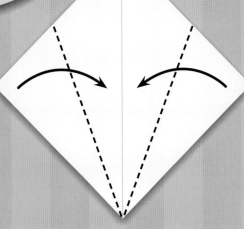

2. Fold in the sides from the bottom corner so that the edges meet in the middle. This makes a kite shape.

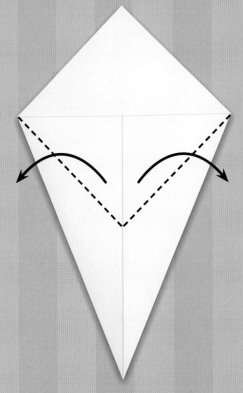

3. Valley fold the flaps on either side. The bottom edges should sit horizontally.

4. Turn the paper over.

Did You Know?

Ghosts are thought of as floating white figures, but there are also stories of ghost trains, phantom ships, and even ghostly animals!

5 Fold in the outer edges as shown.

6 Valley fold the sides from the top point to meet on the central crease.

7 Valley fold the top point down.

8 Make a step fold, starting with a valley fold across the central crease.

9 Turn the model over.

10 Make the ghost's wispy tail with a diagonal valley fold across the bottom point.

11 Your finished project should look like this.

12 Draw the eyes and a wailing mouth. Your origami ghost is ready for some phantom fun! Wooooooo!

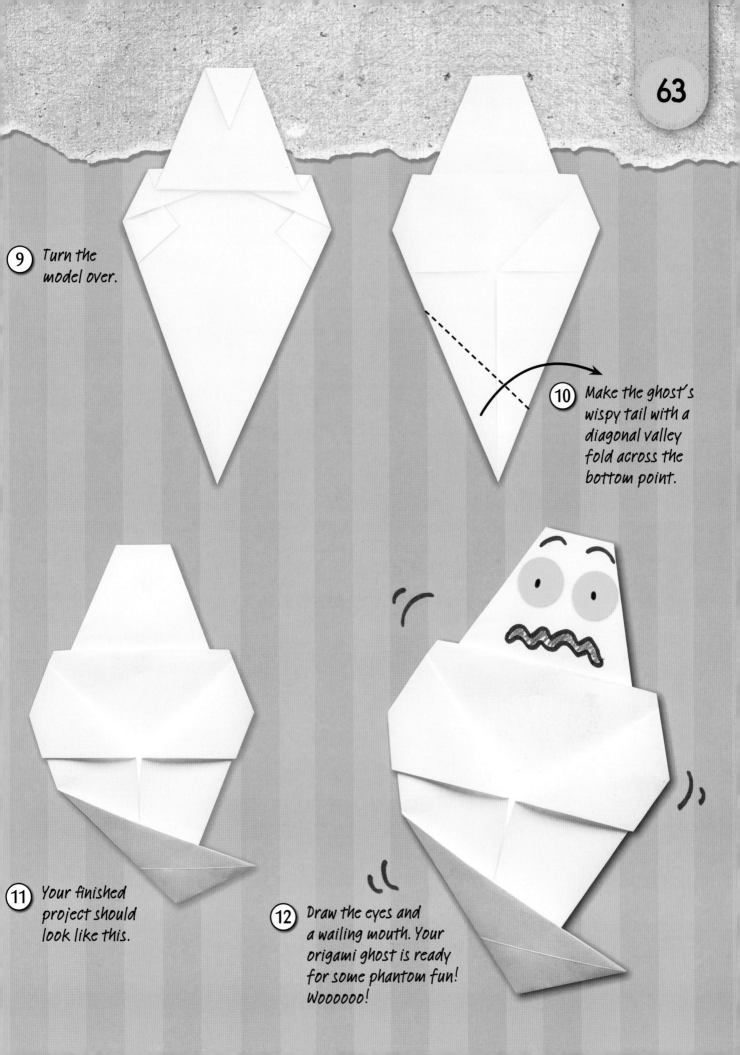

The Gobbler

Look out! The ghastly gobbler is on the prowl for a tasty snack! Follow the steps to fold your own munching menace, then move his giant jaws to make him gobble, guzzle, and gulp!

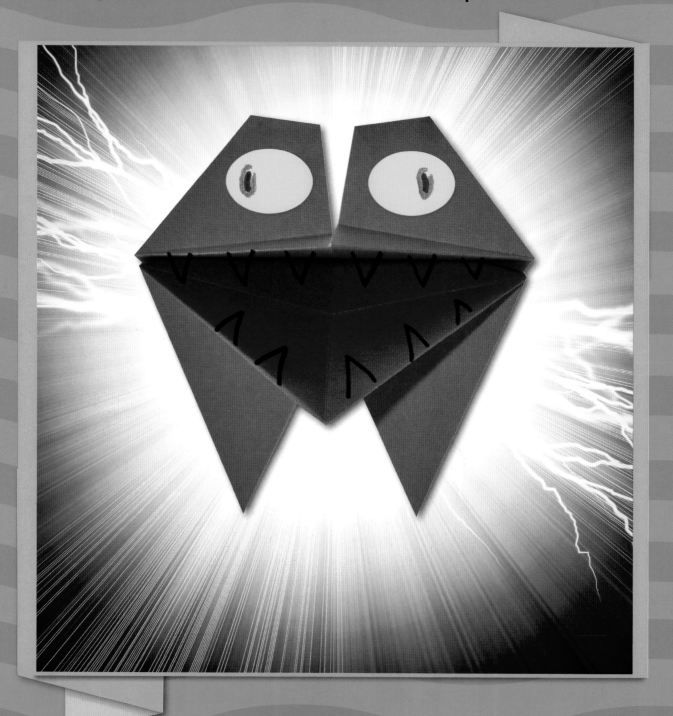

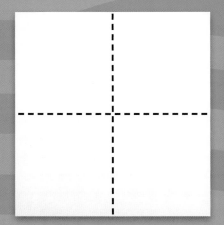

(1) With the paper white side up, fold from top to bottom and unfold, then from left to right and unfold.

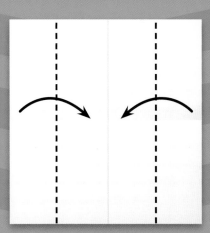

(2) Valley fold the sides to meet the central crease.

(3) Valley fold the top and bottom edges to meet in the middle.

(4) You should have a square. Unfold the top and bottom.

(5) Valley fold the corners to meet the first crease in.

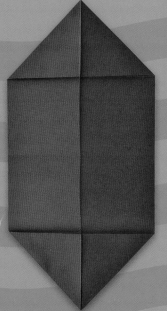

(6) Unfold the corners again.

OPEN

(7) Open up the top left corner.

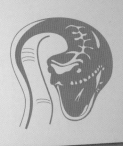

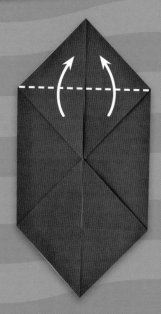

8 Pull the inner point down to the central crease. Press the paper flat to make a triangle.

9 Repeat steps 7 and 8 on the other three corners.

10 Valley fold the flaps at the top.

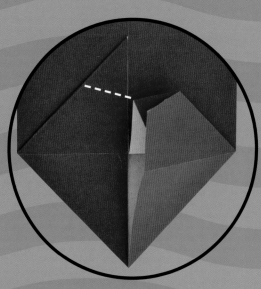

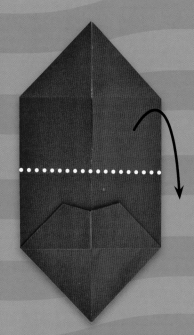

11 Valley fold the points on the bottom flaps, then unfold.

12 Tuck the points in with inside reverse folds.

13 Mountain fold the top half of the paper behind the bottom half.

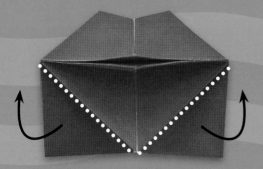

14 Now mountain fold the top behind the point at the bottom.

15 You now have three triangular layers at the bottom. Fold up the top two. These are the lips.

eyes

SIDE VIEW

top lip

folded corners

bottom lip

16 Mountain fold the corners so that they line up with the bottom points.

17 Hold the model by the folded corners and open up the lips. Push in the sides to move the mouth.

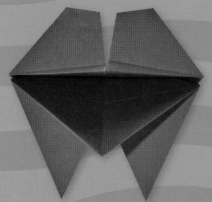

18 Your finished project should look like this.

19 Draw two greedy eyes and a mouth full of sharp teeth. Now your gobbler is ready to guzzle his first meal... but who is on the menu?

Cyclops Eye

Ever get the feeling you're being watched? There's no escaping the gaze of this goggling orb. Follow these steps to create a scary cyclops in the blink of an eye!

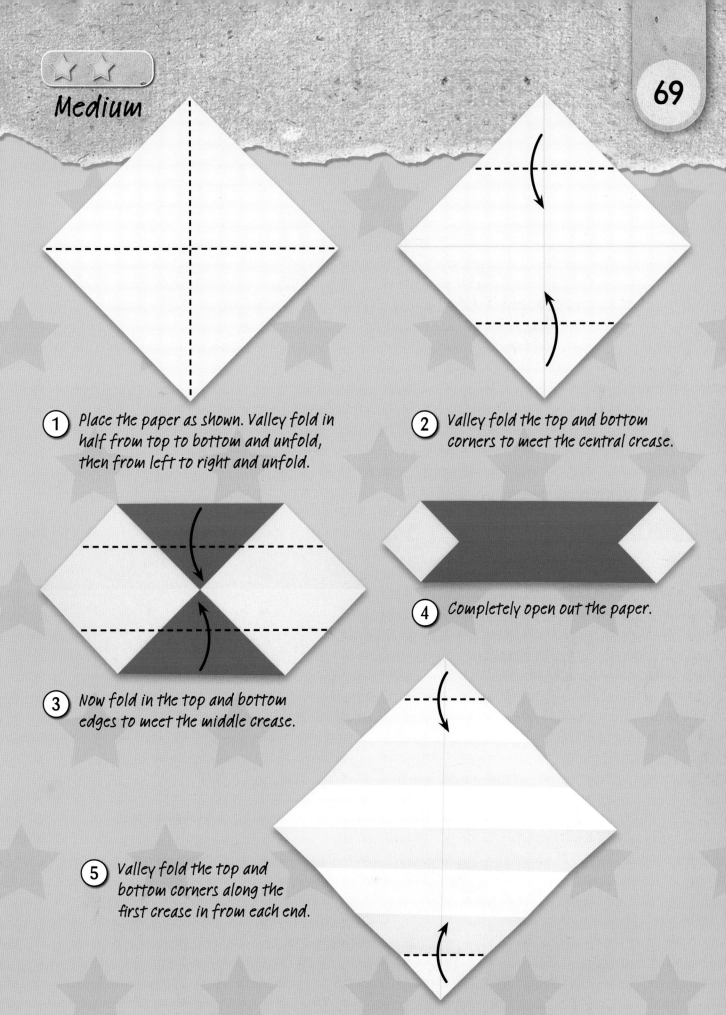

1 Place the paper as shown. Valley fold in half from top to bottom and unfold, then from left to right and unfold.

2 Valley fold the top and bottom corners to meet the central crease.

3 Now fold in the top and bottom edges to meet the middle crease.

4 Completely open out the paper.

5 Valley fold the top and bottom corners along the first crease in from each end.

(6) Fold in the top and bottom along the next crease in.

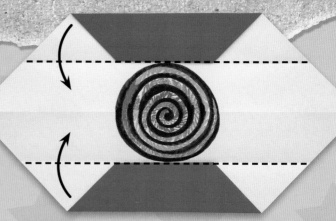

(7) Draw the eye in the middle of the white section. Cover it up again by folding the top and bottom in once more.

(8) Turn the paper over.

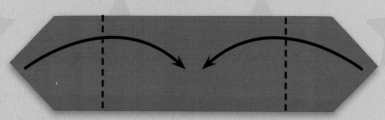

(9) Valley fold the left and right points to meet in the middle.

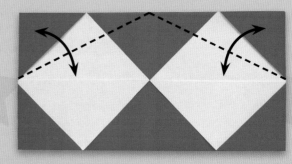

(10) Make angled valley folds across the top half as shown. Crease well, then unfold.

Did You Know?

Ancient Greek myths tell of giants living in caves, each with a single eye in the middle of his forehead. They were called "cyclopes", which means "round-eyed".

11) Make matching folds across the bottom half, and unfold.

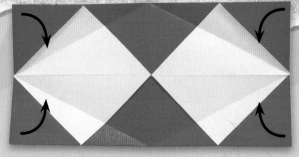

12) Pull the top and bottom corners together on either side.

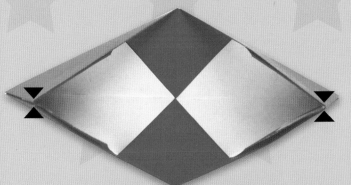

13) Pinch the points between your fingers and turn the model over.

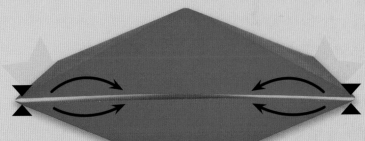

14) Still pinching the points, push in the sides to open up the eye.

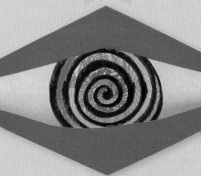

15) Your finished project should look like this.

16) Add some detail to the eerie eyeball and give your friends and family a fright!

Dracula

Watch out! This blood-sucking baddy is searching for his next victim. Take a square of black and white paper and fold this fangtastic vampire with some razor-sharp creases!

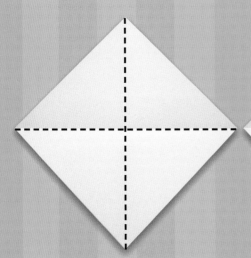

(1) Place the paper as shown. Fold it in half from top to bottom and unfold, then from left to right and unfold.

(2) Valley fold the top point down to meet the central crease.

(3) Valley fold the sides as shown.

(4) Turn the paper over.

(5) Valley fold the sides so that the points meet on the central crease.

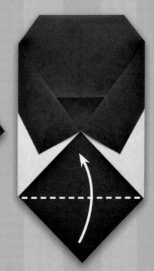

(6) Fold up the bottom point.

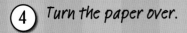

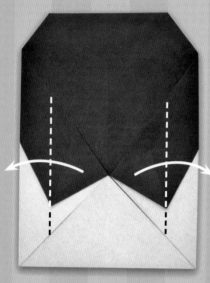
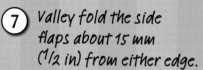

⑦ Valley fold the side flaps about 15 mm (1/2 in) from either edge.

⑧ Your paper should look like this. Undo the folds you just made.

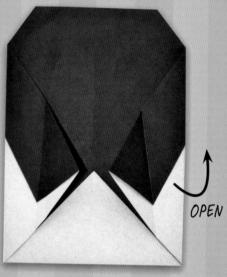

OPEN

⑨ Open up the right flap.

⑩ Take the bottom point on the flap and pull it to the right. Flatten the paper.

⑪ Repeat steps 9 and 10 on the left flap. These points make Dracula's cape collar.

(12) Valley fold the bottom corners.

(13) Turn the model over.

(14) Your finished project should look like this.

(15) Give your Dracula eyes, eyebrows, and a nose. Then add a hungry mouth with frightful fangs!

Nessie

This mysterious Scottish monster is said to live in the deep, dark waters of Loch Ness. This model shows Nessie lifting her head above the water, before she sinks back down below!

① Start with the paper white side up and with one point facing you. Fold it in half from left to right, then unfold.

② Valley fold the sides from the top corner so that the edges meet in the middle. This makes a kite shape.

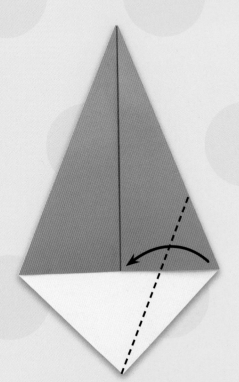

③ Fold in the right point to meet the central crease.

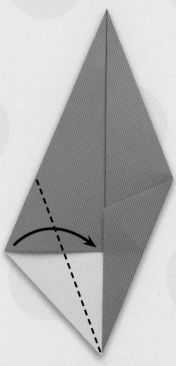

④ Do the same with the left point.

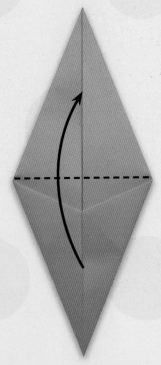

⑤ Valley fold the paper from bottom to top.

Did You Know?

Since 1933, people have reported seeing humps, bumps, and serpent-like shapes in Loch Ness, making Nessie world-famous!

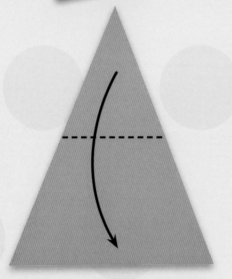

(6) Valley fold the upper layer so that the top point meets the bottom edge.

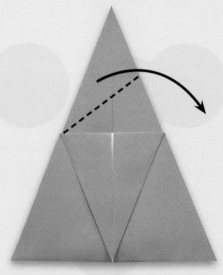

(7) Fold the top point on the lower layer over to the right to make a stretched triangle.

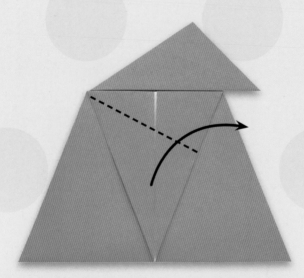

(8) Fold the bottom point over in the same way.

(9) Valley fold the top triangle using the crease you made earlier as a guide.

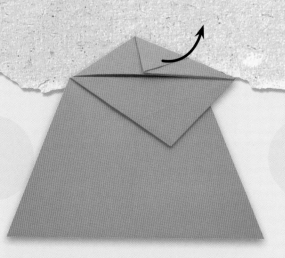

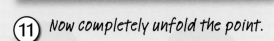

⑩ Open out the fold you just made.

⑪ Now completely unfold the point.

⑬ Fold the paper back down to the stretched triangle shape.

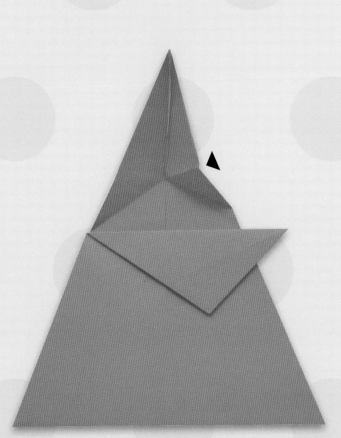

⑫ Make an inside reverse fold, tucking the right edge inside.

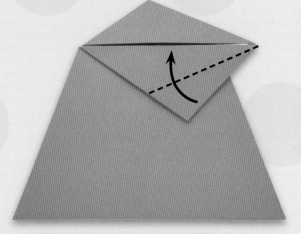

⑭ Now valley fold the lower triangle using the crease you made earlier as a guide.

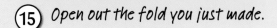

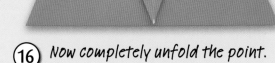

15 Open out the fold you just made.

16 Now completely unfold the point.

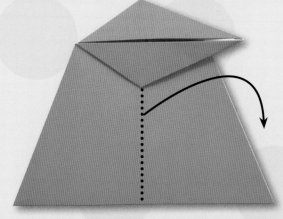

17 Tuck the right edge in with an inside reverse fold. Then fold the paper back down to the stretched triangle shape.

18 The monster's head is complete. Now mountain fold the right side behind the left side to shape the long, thin neck.

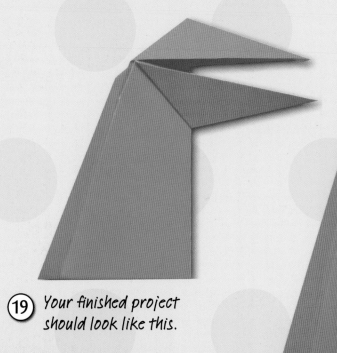

19 Your finished project should look like this.

20 Give her a beady eye. Try sticking Nessie on a piece of paper and draw a lake around this monster of the deep!

Origami on the
MOVE

Car

There are over a billion cars beeping, bumping, and motoring along busy roads all around the world! Make a speedy car of your own with a few fast folds.

1. Starting with the paper white side up, fold it in half from top to bottom and unfold, then from left to right.

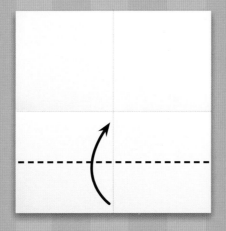

2. Unfold the paper. Valley fold the bottom up to meet the central crease.

3. Now valley fold the right side of the blue strip, as shown.

4. Repeat on the left side.

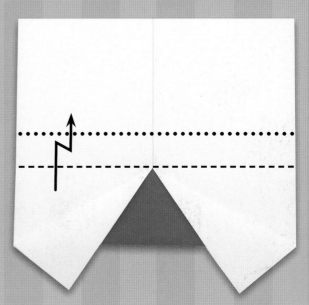

5. Now make a step fold. Valley fold along the central crease and make a mountain fold just above it.

6 Press down on the top section to flatten it.

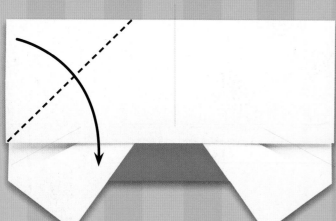

7 Valley fold the top left corner. The point should just meet the lower white edge.

8 Make a smaller valley fold on the top right corner.

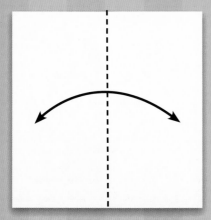

1. Start with the paper white side up. Fold the paper in half from left to right, then unfold.

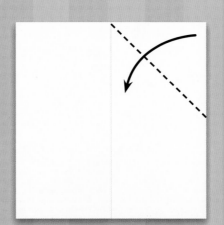

2. Valley fold the right corner so that the top edge meets the central crease.

3. Do the same on the other side.

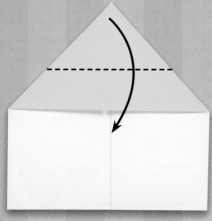

4. Valley fold the point so that the tip comes to around 15 mm (1/2 in) below the yellow section.

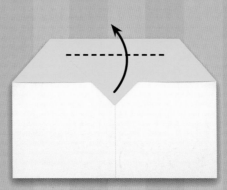

5. Valley fold the point again.

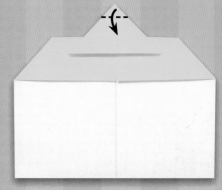

6. Now fold down the tip of the point.

Did You Know?

Wing walkers are people who perform daring feats on the wing of a biplane while it dives, rolls, and flies upside down!

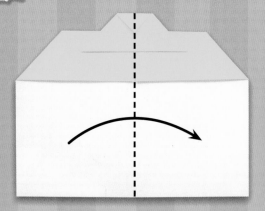

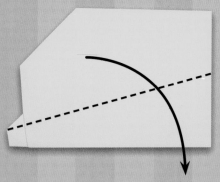

7 Valley fold the paper in half from left to right. Turn the paper on its side.

8 Make a diagonal valley fold across the bottom half of the paper, as shown.

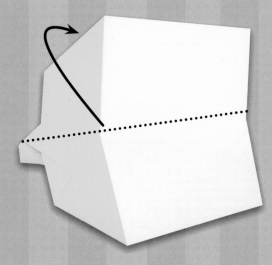

10 Pinch the paper underneath and pull up the wings.

9 Mountain fold the top half of the paper, making the crease line up with the one you made in step 8. These are the wings.

11 Your finished project should look like this.

12 Doodle a pilot onto your finished plane. Then toss it into the air and watch it twirl around and fly back to you!